D1242237

J
954
MAM

Madison County - Canton
Public Library
Madison County Library System

CULTURAL JOURNEYS

TRADITIONS FROM

INDIA

Shelby Mamdani

RAINTREE
STECK-VAUGHN
PUBLISHERS
A Steck-Vaughn Company

Austin, Texas

CULTURAL JOURNEYS

TRADITIONS FROM
AFRICA • THE CARIBBEAN • CHINA • INDIA

Cover: A musician from Rajasthan, India, plays a traditional stringed instrument. The border shows an elephant motif on fabric.

Title page: A woman washes in the watercourse of the world-famous Taj Mahal, in Agra, India.

Contents page: These desert women from Rajasthan have covered their heads with brightly colored scarves.

Index: A group of fishermen from Kerala, India, mending their nets

© Copyright 1999, text, Steck-Vaughn Company

All rights reserved. No part of this book may be reproduced or utilized in any form or by any means, electronic or mechanical, including photocopying, recording, or by any information storage and retrieval system, without permission in writing from the Publisher. Inquiries should be addressed to: Copyright Permissions, Steck-Vaughn Company, P.O. Box 26015, Austin, TX 78755.

Published by Raintree Steck-Vaughn Publishers, an imprint of Steck-Vaughn Company

Library of Congress Cataloging-in-Publication Data
Mamdani, Shelby.
Traditions from India / Shelby Mamdani.
    p.   cm.—(Cultural journeys)
    Includes bibliographical references and index.
    Summary: Discusses a variety of traditions in India and the South Asian countries near it, including food, clothing, music, religions, and festivals.
    ISBN 0-8172-5385-8
    1. South Asia—Civilization—Juvenile literature.
    [1. India—Social life and customs. 2. South Asia—Social life and customs.]
    I. Title. II. Series.
    DS339.M36   1999
    954—dc21   98-23308

Printed in Italy. Bound in the United States.
1 2 3 4 5 6 7 8 9 0 03 02 01 00 99

Picture Acknowledgments:
Chapel Studios 13, (Zul Mukhida), 15 (Bipin Chandra), 14 (Zul Mukhida); Bruce Coleman Limited 4–5 (Kevin Rushby), 6 (Ingo Arndt), 17 (Jules Cowan); David Cumming *contents page*, 29, 36, 37, 40; James Davis Travel Photography *cover* (main picture), 23; Getty Images *title page* (Paul Harris), 7 (Andrew Errington), 8 (Alan Smith), 12 (Philip Reeve), 16 (Paul Harris), 18 (Anthony Cassidy), 19 (Anthony Cassidy), 20 (Andrea Boober), 28 (Anthony Cassidy), 34 (Anthony Cassidy), *index* (David Sutherland); Robert Harding Picture Library 42 (Neil Dyson); Hutchison Library 26; Panos Pictures 14, 22 (Marcus Rose), 33 (Chris Stowers), 39 (Peter Barker); Christine Osbourne Pictures *cover* (border), 21, 30, 35; Ann and Bury Peerless 9, 11, 24, 31, 32; Retna 27 (Bruce Fredericks); Wayland Picture Library 10 (Gordon Clements), 25, 38 (Gordon Clements). The map illustration on page 4 is by Peter Bull. All border artwork for interest boxes is by Pip Adams. The line illustrations for the story are by Helen Holroyd.

CONTENTS

A Land of Extremes

The Indian subcontinent is the home of one of the world's most ancient civilizations. But it is made up of some of the world's youngest nations: India, Pakistan, Bangladesh, and Sri Lanka. The region has a varied landscape, from the highest spot on Earth in the Himalayan Mountains, to the hot, sandy deserts of the northwest. Rain forest covers parts of the northeast, and lush, tropical lands are found in the south. The peninsula has a coast with rocky cliffs, sandy beaches, and wide, calm harbors.

This woman is picking tea, high up on a hillside in Darjeeling, India.

The people of the Indian subcontinent are as varied as its geography. There are about 900 million people living in India alone, giving the country the second-highest population in the world after China. The subcontinent is a place of extremes: of wealth and poverty and of beauty and misery.

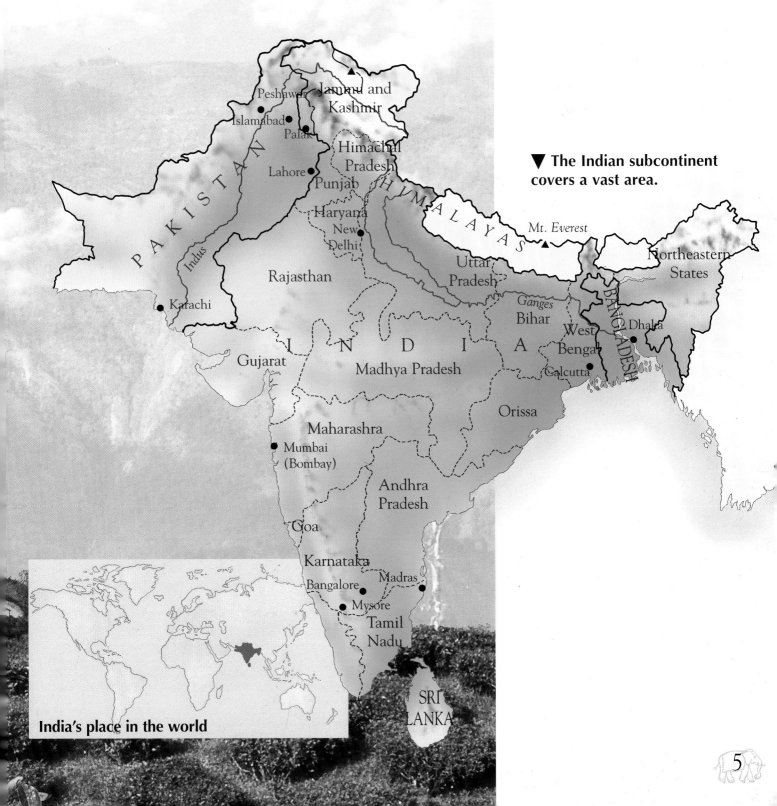

▼ **The Indian subcontinent covers a vast area.**

PAKISTAN

Peshawar
Jammu and Kashmir
Islamabad
Palak
Himachal Pradesh
Lahore
Punjab
HIMALAYAS
Haryana
New Delhi
Indus
Rajasthan
Mt. Everest
Uttar Pradesh
Northeastern States
Karachi
Ganges
Bihar
BANGLADESH
West Bengal
Dhaka
I N D I A
Gujarat
Madhya Pradesh
Calcutta
Orissa
Maharashra
Mumbai (Bombay)
Andhra Pradesh
Goa
Karnataka
Bangalore
Madras
Mysore
Tamil Nadu
SRI LANKA

India's place in the world

India has been invaded by several peoples over nearly 4,000 years, from the ancient Greeks to the descendants of Genghis Khan. During the Mogul period the Muslims influenced parts of Indian culture, and this influence has remained particularly strong in Pakistan and Bangladesh. But India's greatest strength has been its ability to absorb many different cultures and groups of people.

As well as many racial and ethnic groups, the subcontinent has many languages. In India alone there are about 15 official languages and over 800 dialects. But now everyone in India who goes to school studies Hindi and some English.

As a crossroad between East and West, traders and travelers have visited India since ancient times. Sea-going merchants from all over the subcontinent brought their goods and knowledge to other countries around the world. Today, there are thriving communities of people from India living all over Europe, Asia, the Pacific, and North and South America.

Two men lead their horses toward a lake for a drink. This stunning Himalayan landscape is the Shandur Pass in Pakistan.

▼ In the sandy desert area of Rajasthan, India, camels and their riders are a familiar sight.

FOOD AND COOKING

Indian people spend a lot of time visiting each other. Food plays an important part in these social gatherings. People in other parts of the world sometimes think that food in India is called curry. This is a mistake that began when visitors long ago thought that the Tamil word *kari*, meaning a stew dish, was the word for all dishes with sauces. All over the Indian subcontinent, each family mixes its own special blend of spices. These spices are traditionally ground and mixed fresh for each meal. But today, many people grind and store some mixtures in the freezer, to save time.

This spice seller in Fatehpur Sikri, India, has a great variety of pulses and spices for sale.

The subcontinent's climate and geography make it a good place to grow all kinds of spices. Only chilis actually make the food taste hot. The spices give different delicious flavors. During the fifteenth century, European explorers set out to find "the Indies," in search of the valuable spices grown there. But they found the wrong place and ended up in America.

Thousands of chilis drying in the sun. They have been piled high, ready to be put into sacks.

Northern Foods

Food in India can be divided roughly into northern and southern styles of cooking. In Pakistan, Bangladesh, Kashmir, and northern India, the influence of the Muslim Mogul courts that once ruled India has become mixed with Hindu styles of cooking. More meat, especially lamb, is eaten in the north than in the south. People often eat bread with their meals instead of rice there. The bread is usually hand-rolled and baked in clay ovens or on flat griddles. Meat is cooked in underground clay ovens called *tandoors*.

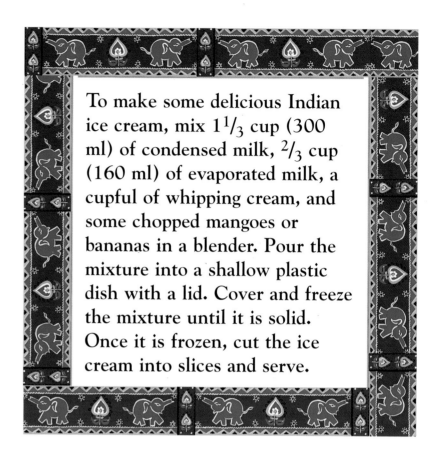

To make some delicious Indian ice cream, mix 1$\frac{1}{3}$ cup (300 ml) of condensed milk, $\frac{2}{3}$ cup (160 ml) of evaporated milk, a cupful of whipping cream, and some chopped mangoes or bananas in a blender. Pour the mixture into a shallow plastic dish with a lid. Cover and freeze the mixture until it is solid. Once it is frozen, cut the ice cream into slices and serve.

This food seller at Clifton Beach, in Pakistan, offers his customers a range of dishes.

There are many types of Indian breads. *Chapati* are eaten at most meals and are made from a mixture of wheat flour, a little oil and water. *Nan* is made from white wheat flour and is soft and puffy, while *paratha* is coated with pure butter, called *ghee*, and is crispy on the outside. There is also very delicate bread, called handkerchief bread, which is rolled very thin and served folded. Handkerchief bread is eaten only on special occasions.

It is polite to eat food with your right hand in India. These people have stopped for a roadside snack in New Delhi, India.

Southern Foods

In southern India and Sri Lanka, the main culture is Hindu. Food in this region is usually strictly vegetarian. But there are many people living on the coast who fish for a living and eat seafood from time to time. Most people in the south have rice with every meal instead of bread. But they do eat special pancakes called *dosas* or *idli*. These are eaten for breakfast or snacks with a vegetable filling and a spicy soup. Some dishes in the south are served on banana leaves instead of plates.

Fishermen in Kerala, India, steer a dugout canoe into the waves in search of fish.

Fruit in southern India and Sri Lanka is varied and delicious. There are many types of fruit, from yellow and green mangoes, and red pomegranates, to payayas and coconuts. People use the juice, or milk, of the coconut, and the flesh, which is grated and added to some dishes or to pickles or chutneys.

Around the World

Indian food has traveled to many parts of the world. Today, Indian restaurants are found in almost every large city. But now it is becoming fashionable for restaurants to specialize in the food of a particular region, because people are learning about the different cooking styles.

A boy samples some of the fruit at a fruit stall in Colombo, Sri Lanka.

13

Food and Religion

This man is making special flat bread for Id ul Fitr.

All over the subcontinent there are special feasts for happy events, such as the birth of a baby or a wedding. There are also forbidden foods or fasts for sad occasions, such as at a death. In Muslim households, the holy month of Ramadan is observed by adults and older children fasting "from the time a thread can be seen in early light until the time it can no longer be seen when the sun goes down." This month marks the time when the prophet Muhammad received the words of God, called the Koran. The month of fasting ends with a festival called Id ul Fitr, when special foods are eaten.

Over three quarters of Indian people are Hindus. Most Hindus do not eat meat. Cows are sacred animals to all Hindus, so beef is forbidden.

In some Hindu families, some of the food that will be eaten each day is placed as an offering in the family's household shrine, to feed the gods.

A Hindu couple makes food offerings in a temple.

CLOTHES AND COSTUME

India is famous for its woven fabrics and embroidery. Cotton, silk, and special wools, such as cashmere, have been made here since very early times.

Cotton and Silk

The earliest cotton in the world was spun and woven in India. Roman emperors wore a delicate cotton from India that they called woven winds. A thousand years later, Mogul emperors named similar fabrics "morning dew" and "cloth of running water." Silk was introduced to India from China. Magnificent brocades woven in India were then traded back to China.

These women in Agra, India, are wearing *saris* decorated with fine gold threads.

Women's Clothes

The *sari*, a length of cotton or silk, is the main garment for most Hindu women in India and Sri Lanka. *Saris* come in thousands of colors and designs, each one typical of a different area. Bright, strong colors are a feature of clothing in much of the subcontinent. Some of the beautiful embroidery on the best *saris* and other clothes is sewn with threads of real gold and silver. Sikh and Muslim women, and women in northern India and Pakistan, traditionally wore a trouser and shirt outfit called a *salwar khamis*. Today, many women of all communities wear the salwar khamis for comfort and freedom of movement.

This *sari* tailor in Nanital, India, is hard at work. He is using a sewing machine, but many *saris* are still made by hand.

17

Men's Clothes

Men in villages in India often wear the *dhoti*, a length of white cotton wrapped around the body, with one or both ends brought through the legs and tucked into the waistband. In northern areas, some men wear the salwar khamis. In the south, men wear a long, wraparound skirt called a *lungi*, which can be worn with or without a shirt. In cities, it is normal to see many men in Western clothing, such as trousers and shirts, or in business suits. For formal occasions, many men choose to wear the classic Indian suit, which has a long, tight-fitting jacket with a high collar.

Light-colored, loose-fitting clothes help these schoolboys keep cool, in Rajasthan, India.

These boys are wearing headdresses made from a piece of material. They come in a variety of colors.

Children's Clothes

Children usually wear Western-style clothing. But on special occasions, they may wear smaller versions of traditional adult clothing.

Special Occasions

Henna designs can be very complicated. This woman's hand has just been painted for a wedding ceremony.

Weddings are very important occasions. In Gujarat and Kashmir, the bride wears a *gagrah choli*, a heavily embroidered outfit with a full, circular skirt, a jacket, and a veil. In Muslim and Hindu families, the night before the wedding, the bride's sisters paint beautiful designs on her hands and feet with *Mehndi*, a paste made from the henna plant. When the bride washes the next morning, the design turns from black to bright red, a color that brings good luck. For the ceremony, the bride wears gold jewelry and a beautiful red *sari*, heavily embroidered with gold.

Make your own Mehndi designs, without getting messy. With a felt-tip pen draw around your hands onto some cardboard. Cut out the hands. With the felt-tip pen, draw patterns all over the cardboard hands. You can make each one different.

If the groom is from a rich family, he rides to the house of the bride on the back of a horse or an elephant. But most grooms arrive in a decorated car, accompanied by friends, family, and musicians. Both the bride and the groom wear garlands of flowers, given by the bride's family. Marigolds are traditionally sacred flowers for Hindus, and jasmine or roses are special for Muslim couples. Nowadays, many kinds of flowers are used.

This Muslim couple are dressed in their finest clothes for their wedding ceremony in Karachi, Pakistan.

MUSIC AND DANCE

Music is an important part of Indian life. Both music and dance have been closely tied to religion since ancient times. Making and playing music and dancing were traditionally part of offerings made to the gods. The term for music in Hindi originally included music, dance, and drama all together. It is only modern music that separates each of these skills.

Musicians play at a sports festival in Pakistan.

Classical Music

Classical music is performed with the musicians seated on the floor. The music played in the south of the subcontinent may be played on stringed instruments called *vina* or *tempura*. Other instruments from this area are the *veenu*, a kind of flute, and the *mrdangam*, a southern drum. In the north, the influence of the Muslim cultures of Turkey and Persia can be seen in the music. Here, the *sitar*, a large stringed instrument, and the *tabla*, two drums, are accompanied by the *sarangi*, a single-stringed instrument played with a bow, and the *shehnai*, which is similar to an oboe.

This musician in Rajasthan, India, is playing a traditional stringed instrument.

Folk Dance and Drama

According to ancient Hindu texts, classical dance was given to humans by the god Shiva in his form as Shiva Nataraja, "Lord of the Dance." *Bharat Natyam* is an important dance that is usually performed by a woman. The dancer tells stories of the gods, using facial expressions, hand gestures, and body poses that have been taught for thousands of years. The dancer wears ankle bracelets with bells attached. The bells make a lovely sound to accompany the music as the dancer makes each step. Dancers wear flowers in their hair, and henna is painted on their hands and feet.

A group of Manipuri dancers performs in Bangladesh.

A girl from Assam, India, plays her drum for a lively dance.

There are many other forms of classical dance. Manipuri is a graceful style of dance from eastern India. The dances tell the story of the god Krishna's moonlight dance with the cowherd maidens, when each one thought she danced with him alone. *Kathakali* dances, from Kerala, in India, are dance dramas that began during the seventeenth century. The word *kathakali* means "story play." The plays are often performed outside and may last all night.

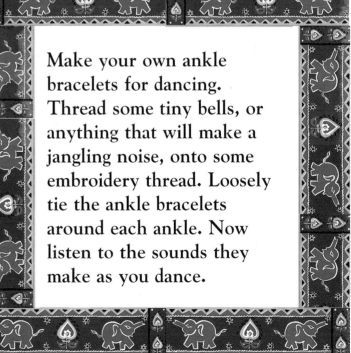

Make your own ankle bracelets for dancing. Thread some tiny bells, or anything that will make a jangling noise, onto some embroidery thread. Loosely tie the ankle bracelets around each ankle. Now listen to the sounds they make as you dance.

Indian Music Around the World

Indian music has traveled all around the world. Over thirty years ago, a famous rock group from Liverpool, England, called the Beatles, used *sitar* music in some of their hit songs. More recently, the group Kula Shaker has used Indian music styles in their songs.

This musician is playing an instrument called a *sitar*. Sitars are used in some modern popular music.

Members of the British group, Kula Shaker, collect an award for their music.

Bhangra-pop music was first made popular outside India by British-born musicians in the group *Apache Indian*, who mixed Punjabi music with Afro-Caribbean and Western styles.

Modern Indian dancers, such as Malika Sarubai, trained in the classical tradition, but have performed modern pieces in cities all over the world.

RELIGION AND FESTIVALS

India is the birthplace of several religions—Hinduism, Buddhism, Jainism, and Sikhism. But other religions, such as Islam, Christianity, Judaism, and Zoroastrianism, have traveled to the subcontinent from other parts of the world. In spite of these different beliefs, most of the people of these faiths have lived side by side and learned from one another.

About 85 percent of the Indian population is Hindu. This ancient religion began more than 3,000 years ago. Hindus believe in one supreme being, Brahman, the high god, who takes on three main forms: Brahma the Creator, Vishnu the Preserver, and Shiva the Destroyer. Vishnu and Shiva are believed to come to Earth in human or animal forms called avatars. There are many other gods and goddesses, but Hindus believe that these gods are all part of the supreme Brahman.

These Brahman Hindus are praying before eating.

One of the most popular avatars of Vishnu is Krishna, the blue god of love. Rama is another avatar of Vishnu, who represents duty and courage. The elephant-headed god Ganesha is the Lord of Beginnings and the Remover of Obstacles. He also brings good luck and is especially important to people in business and at weddings.

The Ganges River is sacred to Hindus, who believe the river has the power to take away sins.

Buddhism

During the fifth century B.C., Prince Siddhartha Gautama founded Buddhism. He gave up his life in a palace and went to live among the poor, seeking the truth through meditation and prayer. Eventually he found salvation, and after his death he was called The Buddha, which means "the enlightened one." There are very few Buddhists in India today, but Buddhism has become a major religion in Southern and Southeast Asia.

Islam

Islam came to the subcontinent around the year A.D. 711. Followers of Islam are called Muslims. Muslims believe that the word of God was revealed to the prophet Muhammed in the city of Mecca in Saudi Arabia. Today, there are nearly 90 million Muslims in India, and Pakistan and Bangladesh are Islamic states.

These Muslim boys in Pakistan are reading the Koran, the holy book of Islam.

Sikhism

During the sixteenth century, Guru Nanak founded a new religion. His followers are called Sikhs, which means "disciples." Sikhism teaches that there is only one God, and that hard work, honesty, and equality are important. Around 15 million Sikhs live in India, mainly in the Punjab, and many more have settled in other countries around the world.

The Golden Temple at Amritsar, in India, is one of the most important and well-known places of worship, or *gurdwaras*, for Sikhs.

Celebrations

There are several Hindu calendars. The most common one is lunar. Each month in the lunar calendar is the gap between two new moons. This means that festivals are not held on the same day each year.

Raksha Bandhan is a festival for brothers and sisters, which takes place in July or August, mainly in the north and west of India. At this time, girls make *rakhi*, good luck bracelets made of silken or cotton threads, and tie them on the wrists of male relatives. This tradition is based on the story of the wife of the god Indra, who tied a rakhi around his wrist for luck before he battled with a demon.

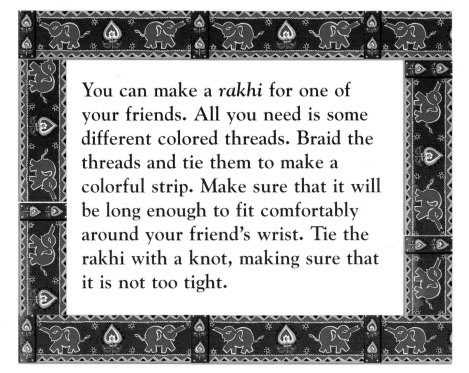

You can make a *rakhi* for one of your friends. All you need is some different colored threads. Braid the threads and tie them to make a colorful strip. Make sure that it will be long enough to fit comfortably around your friend's wrist. Tie the rakhi with a knot, making sure that it is not too tight.

Sometimes called the festival of color, *Holi* marks the coming of spring. Hindu people throw colored powders and water over each other.

Fireworks are an important part of *Diwali* celebrations.

Diwali is celebrated in October or November. It means "garland of lights," and it is actually several festivals in one. In some parts of India, it is the festival of the goddess Lakshmi, the giver of wealth and good luck. In Bengal, Kali, the goddess of destruction, is worshiped. In villages, women draw *rangoli* on the floor near the door to lure the goddess to their house. These are beautiful designs drawn with colored powders or dyes. During *Diwali*, people decorate their houses with oil or electric lights, to celebrate the safe return of Rama after rescuing his wife Sita from the demon king Ravana. Most Hindus around the world send cards to friends and relations and exchange gifts to mark the season.

Dassehra is a Hindu festival in September and October. At this festival people worship three goddesses, Navaratri, Durga and Puja, who are all forms of the same female power, Shakti. In Gujarat, women dance together in a circle, called the *dandia ras*, hitting sticks together as they move. In Bengal, the image of Durga, a form of the goddess who saved the earth from a demon bull, is celebrated.

In other areas, people celebrate the victory of Rama over the demon Ravana. Dramas of the fierce battle between them are performed over the nine nights of the festival.

Beautifully decorated elephants and their riders parade through the streets of Mysore, India, for the *Dassehra* festival.

For Muslims, the most important festivals are *Id ul Fitr*, at the end of the month of fasting, and *Id ul Haj*, at the end of the month of pilgrimage. At these times, Muslim families celebrate with special foods and new clothes and visit each other to exchange gifts and good wishes.

The festival of *Basant* is shared by Hindus and Sikhs in India and Pakistan, to mark the coming of spring. *Basant* is held in January or February. Everyone wears yellow, which is the color of spring in India. Kite-flying competitions are also part of the celebrations.

These people have dressed up to take part in some festival dancing during *Id ul Fitr*.

HAVING FUN

Sports, such as wrestling and games with dice, are mentioned in the ancient stories, the *Mahabharata* and the *Ramayana*. They have been played for more than 3,000 years. Chess was originally a military game, where the pieces represented elephants, horses, foot soldiers, and generals. After chess spread to Persia and Europe, the pieces changed into the knights, rooks, pawns, and bishops that are part of the modern game. A game of dice begins the story of the *Mahabharata* and sets off a series of adventures and great battles.

These children in Sri Lanka are playing a simple board game called *carom*.

Camel racing is a fast and furious sport in Rajasthan, India.

Religious Games

Some Indian games have religious backgrounds. Snakes and ladders was originally a Hindu game, called *moksha-pettamu*. The snakes represented the temptation of evil, and the ladders helped players on their way to heaven. Today, the game is popular in many parts of the world.

Cricket

If any sport can be named as the national sport, it has to be cricket. It was introduced to the subcontinent when India belonged to the British Empire. Cricket is the favorite sport for people of all ages throughout the subcontinent. Three-day matches, or cricket tests, especially between the national teams, draw huge crowds. Even in rural areas, people gather to listen to village radio or television sets to support their teams. Indians are enthusiastic about sports, and many wealthy families in city areas belong to clubs where they can play tennis, badminton, and other sports.

Cricket is a popular sport on summer evenings in Pakistan.

A movie advertisement in Calcutta, India. Going to the movies is a very popular form of entertainment all over the subcontinent.

Movies

India has the world's largest film industry, and people love to go to the movies, wherever they live. Most Indian films are stories about love and hate or good and evil. They are full of colorful dances, singing, and glamorous film stars wearing spectacular costumes. Each day, over 70 million people go to the movies in India. The city of Mumbai (known as Bombay until 1995), has even been nicknamed Bollywood, because its film industry is as important as Hollywood.

Children's Games

Many children in the Indian subcontinent have to work with the rest of their families so that they can afford to buy basic things, such as food and clothing. They do not have much time to play, and many do not go to school. But there are many festivals in India—over thirty major ones, and children enjoy these celebrations and the activities that are connected with them.

Two teams of young people in India battle for each other's territory in the popular game of *Kabadi*.

This boy in Sri Lanka is trying out his homemade go-cart. It is made from pieces of wood and string.

Children all around the subcontinent also play simple games, using homemade toys, such as tops, hobbyhorses, and hoops.

Circle games are especially popular, such as *Kokla-chaupakee*, which is played by some groups of children in Pakistan. The rules have been written here for you to try.

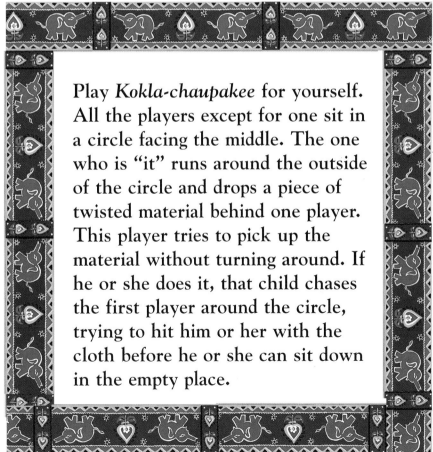

Play *Kokla-chaupakee* for yourself. All the players except for one sit in a circle facing the middle. The one who is "it" runs around the outside of the circle and drops a piece of twisted material behind one player. This player tries to pick up the material without turning around. If he or she does it, that child chases the first player around the circle, trying to hit him or her with the cloth before he or she can sit down in the empty place.

STORY TIME

The greatest books in India were originally stories memorized and sung or chanted aloud. The *Mahabharata*, which is over 100,000 verses long, is the longest book in the world. It is the story of the great battle between two groups of cousins, the five royal Pandava brothers and their hundred Kaurava cousins, who fought to control ancient India. Within the main tale are many smaller episodes about the adventures of the Pandava princes. This ancient story has entertained people in India for centuries and is still popular today.

THE THOUSAND-PETALED LOTUS
An Episode from *The Mahabharata*

After losing their kingdom to the Kaurava cousins, and agreeing to live for fourteen years in the wilderness, the Pandava brothers wandered far away to Kailasa Mountain in the Himalayas, the highest place on Earth. There they looked for the castle of King Vaishravana, who controlled great wealth and treasures. The land of Kailasa was high grassland, with great trees that had fruits and fragrant blossoms. The waterfalls, rivers, and lakes were filled with lotus blossoms, swans, and wild geese. There were mountains of gold and jewels, and trees with silver leaves, and caves that glowed red inside.

In this place, Draupadi, Queen of the Pandavas, was sitting one morning when the wind blew a most beautiful flower into her lap: a fragrant white lotus with a thousand petals. She carried it to her husband and said, "If I only had more flowers like this, I could make our humble home of branches and leaves look so much more beautiful. Please bring more like this to me."

"I will," promised her husband, Bhima.

So Bhima went to search through the forests and the fields, looking for the place where the thousand-petaled lotus grew. After a while, he came to a place where the road was blocked by a sleeping monkey.

"Out of the way, monkey!" said Bhima. "Let me pass!"

The monkey opened one eye and looked at Bhima. "Have you no manners? I was just taking a little nap, and even though I am only an animal, you didn't have to wake me up, did you?"

"Just move aside," said Bhima, impatiently. "I'm in a great hurry."

"You might as well give up," said the monkey. "This road leads to heaven, and only the gods are allowed to use it. I'm only trying to help you, for if you try to pass me, you will be in big trouble!"

At this point, Bhima became very impatient. He grabbed the monkey by the tail, to pull him out of the way, but he couldn't move it! He pulled, and pulled, and pulled again, but in spite of all his strength, he couldn't move the creature.

"Oh, Son of the Wind," said the monkey (for Bhima's father was the Wind God) "don't you recognize me?"

And suddenly Bhima knew that this was no ordinary monkey, but Hanuman, the Monkey King, and he bowed and apologized, "Hanuman, my brother!" For Hanuman was a great general and warrior, like Bhima himself. He said to Hanuman, "Why are you here? And what are you doing?"

"I am enjoying being a monkey, chasing everything, but catching nothing because I am always catching sight of something new to chase before I catch the last thing! All the time running and leaping, and never having to worry about owning anything—that's the life for me! Oh, and by the way, the lotus lake is just over there." And he pointed over Bhima's shoulder.

Soon, Bhima stood near the gate of King Vaishravana's castle, which stood next to the lake where the thousand-petaled lotus flower grew. It was a castle of gold and crystal, of jewels and pearls, of silver and ivory, of diamonds and turquoise, and jewels beyond description. And although it was all the wealth that men could desire, yet the flower of the lotus was more beautiful still.

Inside the castle, King Vaishravana was losing his temper.

"What?" he thundered. "A man has discovered the castle? He must die! No one must know where my castle lies!"

He leapt into his chariot of dark clouds, which was bound together by rainbows tied in colorful knots. Eighteen thousand horses pulled the chariot into the sky, and the city along with it, until they were floating on the air right over Bhima. Leaning his head out of the chariot, King Vaishravana called down, "Who are you? How dare you come here to my land?"

"I am looking for flowers," said Bhima softly.

"WHAT?" screeched the King. "You haven't come to rob me?"

"All that you own means nothing to the birds in the trees and the animals of the forest. I have come for the lovely thousand-petaled lotus with the sweetest perfume on Earth. My wife, Draupadi, has asked this of me. How can I disappoint her?"

Still, King Vaishravana shouted and ranted.

Finally, Bhima said "Beware, O King, I am Bhima, Son of the Wind." The king saw that Bhima was stronger than all of his soldiers.

"Bhima, I give you the flowers with all my heart," replied the king. He ordered his general to fill Bhima's arms with the fragrant blossoms. "Take this gift for Draupadi, and take also my promise of friendship and protection. While you and your family still wander the world, I will guard you." Then the king turned his horses, and returned to the castle. And Bhima listened to his father, the Wind, move through the valley and up the mountain. He knew that soon he, Draupadi, and the rest of his family would cease their wandering and return to the world.

GLOSSARY

Avatars Different forms of the same god.

Brocades Silk cloths with raised patterns.

Cashmere A very soft, silky woolen material.

Ethnic groups Small groups of people whose racial or cultural background is different from the main population.

Griddle A flat, heated pan, used for cooking.

Henna A type of plant that produces a natural dye.

Lotus A beautiful flower that blooms in water.

Lunar Based on the moon.

Meditation Deep and continued thought.

Merchants Traders who buy and sell foreign goods.

Mogul A name given to the period of Muslim rule in India from the sixteenth to the nineteenth centuries.

Peninsula A piece of land that is almost surrounded by water.

Pilgrimage A journey made to a holy place for spiritual reasons.

Rain forest A forest found in tropical areas, with very high rainfall.

Salvation Being freed from sin and allowed entry to heaven.

Shrine A casket for holding holy or sacred items.

Subcontinent A large land area, smaller than and independent of its continent.

FURTHER INFORMATION

Books to Read:

Brace, Steve. *Bangladesh* (Enchantment of the World). Austin, TX: Thomson Learning, 1995.

Cumming, David. *The Ganges Delta and Its People* (People and Places). Austin, TX: Thomson Learning, 1994.

———. *India* (Economically Developing Countries). Austin, TX: Thomson Learning, 1995.

Dhanjal, Beryl. *Amritsar* (Holy Cities). Parsippany, NJ: Dillon Press, 1994.

Ganeri, Anita. *Exploration into India* (Exploration Into). Parsippany, NJ: New Discovery, 1995.

———. *India* (Country Fact Files). Austin, TX: Raintree Steck-Vaughn, 1995.

———. *India* (Country Topics for Crafts Projects). Danbury, CT: Franklin Watts, 1994.

Hermes, Jules M. *The Children of India* (The World's Children). Minneapolis, MN: Carolrhoda, 1993.

Kagda, Falaq. *India* (Festivals of the World). Milwaukee, WI: Gareth Stevens, 1997.

Khan, Eaniqa and Rob Unwin. *Pakistan* (Country Insights). Austin, TX: Raintree Steck-Vaughn, 1997.

INDEX

Page numbers in **bold** refer to photographs.

© Copyright 1998 Wayland (Publishers) Ltd.

Madison County - Canton
Public Library
Madison County Library System